TARA
LIPINSKI

BY RICHARD RAMBECK

(Photo on front cover)

USA's Tara Lipinski performs her routine at the White Ring Arena in Nagano, Japan. February 20, 1998.

(Photo on previous pages)

Gold medalist Tara Lipinski, center, silver medalist Michelle Kwan, left, and bronze medalist Vanessa Gusmeroli of France at the World Figure Skating Championships in Lausanne, Switzerland. March 22, 1997.

GRAPHIC DESIGN
Robert A. Honey, Seattle

PHOTO RESEARCH
James R. Rothaus, James R. Rothaus & Associates

ELECTRONIC PRE-PRESS PRODUCTION
Robert E. Bonaker, Graphic Design & Consulting Co.

PHOTOGRAPHY
All photos by Associated Press AP

Library of Congress Cataloging-in-Publication Data
Rambeck, Richard
Tara Lipinski / by Richard Rambeck
p. cm.
Summary: A brief biography of the youngest skater ever to win United States and World Figure Skating Championships and go on to win a gold medal in the 1998 Winter Olympics.
ISBN 1-56766-525-5 (library : reinforced : alk. paper)

1. Lipinski, Tara, 1982- — Juvenile literature.
2. Skaters—United States—Biography—Juvenile literature.
[1. Lipinski, Tara 1982- . 2. Figure skaters. 3. Women—Biography.]
I. Title
GV850.J56R36 1998   98-6785
796.91'2'092 — dc21   CIP
[B]   AC

CONTENTS